Preparation guide for
Mentors & Volunteers

WORKING
WITH OUR
YOUTH

JAMEL BRAGG

Note: This book is being provided as a resource to organizations and groups that are out to make a direct impact on Working with our Youth. If you are such an entity please email us at info@prestigecommunicationgroup.com so we can provide you with a free copy..

Published by:
Prestige Communication Group, LLC
PO Box 1129
New York, NY 10027

ISBN-13: 978-1496102676
ISBN-10: 1496102673

Edited by: Salih Israil

This is the opinion of the author and is for reference purposes only.

ACKNOWLEDGEMENT

LIFE, you have shown me that Change is possible, just as long as I was willing to accept and commit myself to it. Throughout the years we have had some real rough times, in which I'm not proud of, but you have sent some amazing people in my life, to make that transition possible.

To Prestige Communication Group, thank you for taking the chance and giving me the opportunity to be heard.

Thank you to the readers it shows that you are willing to roll up your sleeves and assist with the crisis on our hands of saving our youths.

Table of Contents

Introduction

Today, we talk about troubled youth as if they magically fall out the sky like raindrops. It's as if they're mysteriously popping up all across the country. If you watch the news or listen to political pundits, it would appear that the only thing we can say for sure is that a large majority of the youth in this country is troubled and we're scrambling as a nation to find a way to address this horrifying reality. Experts have a lot to say about the problem. Unfortunately, they talk about the problem in terms of a breakdown of certain formal and informal institutional structures, such as the school system, the family, and the community as a whole. While there may be some value in their assessments and proposed approaches to solving the problem, their insight and their suggestions are framed by the statistical representations of the problem. This is not a bad thing, nor am I saying their approaches can't prove fruitful.

However, I am saying that the majority of their suggestions and solutions result in a **top-down approach**. Their suggestions usually involve a change in how we're doing things at the institutional level, changes that usually stir up moral, economic, and political controversy and take years to get approved and implemented. We've recently seen a few initiatives to implement these institutional changes: force a change in the family institution by charging parents for the violations of their children, force a change in the school system by increasing the role and presence of law enforcement officers at schools, force a change in the community by having marches against youth violence. Again, I'm not saying any of these efforts are useless. I'm saying they're all aimed at addressing the notion, the question, and the problem of troubled youth. That's all good, but all of that is meaningless if each and every one of us who are concerned with this very important issue don't do our part in a **bottom-up approach**.

There is no doubt that the number of children in this country that qualify as troubled youth is staggering, and that number is growing exponentially. Those statistics represent our sons, daughters, brothers, sisters, nieces, nephews, cousins, friends, and neighbors. They are youths we interact with every day. Those statistics represent youth that may be a terror or disrespectful to someone else but caring and perfectly respectful to us. Long before troubled youth get into serious trouble, we have a variety of opportunities to have a positive influence on them, opportunities that could alter their lives for the better. Unfortunately, many of us don't realize there are such opportunities and/or simply don't know how to make the best of them. We often take our cue from the experts and get caught up in looking at the issue of troubled youth like a never-ending forest. We convince ourselves that we're not equipped or qualified to make a difference.

Well, this is not a book for experts and professionals such as policy makers and social workers. This is a simple and easy to read guide to help everyday people identify the best ways for them to get involved with our youth.

"EVERY INTERSECTION IN THE ROAD OF LIFE, IS AN OPPORTUNITY TO MAKE A DECISION."

DUKE ELLINGTON

Tip One: Know Your "Why"

There are many ways to get involved with helping the youth. It can be something as formal as becoming a volunteer at your local Boys and Girls Club or something as informal as taking time out of your busy life a few times a week to lend an ear or give advice to a young neighbor. No matter what you decide to do to engage our youth, the reasons that drive you to do it will have a serious impact on how you do it. That's why it is very important for you to know and understand your motives for getting involved.

While this may sound trivial, knowing and understanding your motives may very well be the most important step you take in helping. Unfortunately, it's something many of us take for granted. I mean, as long as we're involved, why should our motives matter? What's important is that we reach out and get active with our youth, right? Wrong.

At the heart of the question of our motives is the question of sincerity. Sincerity is a crucial element of dealing with our youth. You may find yourself in a position to give some youth the most important piece of advice they will ever hear, they may be receptive to what it is you have to say, but the moment they pick up on an inkling of insincerity the opportunity is in serious danger of being wasted. Think about it.

How often does the issue of someone's motives affect how we receive their message? If we look at politicians for example, they often will make promises that sound good. The problem is their track records and affiliations sometimes create doubts as to their motives for their positions on certain issues, which often lead us to feel like they're only saying what they think we want to hear, and that makes us skeptical about their motives. That skepticism usually results in our refusal to take them seriously on any issue. Well, our youth react to us pretty much the same way. They can become skeptical of our motives and lose all confidence in everything we try to tell or show them.

When it comes to the question of sincerity, many of our youth have become experts at spotting when the actions of so-called helpers don't match up with how those helpers really feel. But this should come as no surprise. Our youth are constantly in contact with teachers, social workers, afterschool program staff, and other professionals that interact with them for the sole purpose of getting a paycheck. Although there is nothing inherently wrong with these professionals having a pay-check motive, that motive shines through in how they deal with the youth. Our youth pick up on these motives and begin to view these professionals with a skeptical eye. Now a situation could arise where one of these professionals attempt to give a youth some powerful advice or guidance however, a breakdown in how the youth understands the professional's motives and what the professional is attempting to convey, there's a strong possibility that the youth won't be receptive.

The idea of knowing and understanding your reasons and motives for working with our youth is not to suggest that there are right or wrong motives or reasons. This is not about passing judgment. It's about acknowledging that your reasons and motives for getting involved with working with our youth will influence, dictate, and/or set the **limits of your involvement.** The limits of your involvement have a direct impact on shaping your expectations for working with youth and the youth's expectations of you.

Knowing and understanding why you're getting involved allows you to get a general idea of your level of involvement and lets you prepare for how to handle those situations that may call for more than you're willing to do. Knowing your limits of involvement allows you to focus on getting the most out of what you're willing to do. There are good teachers who work with youth for the purpose of getting a paycheck, they do so without expecting to have to do anything beyond what is clearly laid out in their job description as teachers.

Surprisingly, they also do their jobs with a high level of commitment and dedication without fostering false expectations in their students. You see, the fact that they know and understand that they're primarily there for a paycheck allows them to set limitations on their involvement with students. The very presence of these limits of involvement help them stay focused on their jobs and prepared for situations where these limits are approached. In the event that they find themselves in a situation where a student requests or requires more than what is laid out in their job description. They're prepared to professionally and respectfully defuse the situation without alienating the student. This allows them to maintain students' confidence in those areas that do fall within their job description while they avoid doing anything that falls outside of their job description.

Even if a teacher is motivated by more than earning a paycheck, he/she still has to set limits of involvement with their students and be prepared to respond appropriately when those limits are approached. They must do this in a way that doesn't destroy their students' confidence in them.

No matter which role you choose to play in working with our youth, no matter which youth you decided to work with, you need to give some serious thought to why you're getting involved in working with them. Be very clear about how much you're willing to do in your work. Set your limits of involvement before you start getting involved, even if those limits are only tentative. Despite how our so-called troubled youth are depicted in the media, they are very smart, cunning, and creative. You need to respond in ways that don't undermine the limit of involvement you've set for yourself while simultaneously maintaining the youths' confidence in you.

For example, let's say you sign up at the community center as a volunteer driver for a six-member youth bowling team. You're willing to transport the team to the bowling alley and back twice a week and cover the gas costs. You've squeezed these two times a week out of your busy schedule and made a commitment to sacrifice those gas costs from your budget because you've decided to get involved by helping youth do something fun and constructive.

After about two months of doing this, you develop a nice rapport with the youth. The drives back and forth provide a great opportunity for you to engage them in all kinds of conversations about a wide range of topics: school, family, life-goals, relationships, dealing with confrontations, to name a few. Then one day, after dropping the team off at the center, two of them pull you aside with a request. This request clearly requires you to go beyond the limit of involvement you've set for yourself.

So, how should you respond? Well, if you didn't seriously consider your motives for being involved with the bowling team and you didn't get a clear understanding of what your limits of involvement would be, you're probably going to say whatever comes to mind to get you out of such an awkward situation, maybe come up with some kind of excuse. They'll sense your insincerity, you'll lose their trust in you and any opportunity you could've had to have a positive influence on them.

However, if you gave serious thought to why you were getting involved before you got involved with them, and you came up with a clear idea of what your limits of involvement would be, your response will come naturally and from the heart. Even if it is not the response the two youth are looking for, it will come off sincere and won't damage their confidence in you in the least.

As I said, knowing and understanding your motives for working with our youth may very well be the most important step you take in helping our youth. If you're seriously considering working with our youth don't take this step lightly. Know and understand why you're getting involved and be crystal clear about how much you're willing to do.

If we look at why some people got involved they vary. It could be just as simple as a team needs a coach. A personal conviction because they have personally gone through a trauma and would like to avoid it happening to another. Another may just want to be of service by giving their time, skill or resources.

There are many "whys" and reasons for taking on this work. Whether it's a particular youth in need, or a collective group you are looking to assist, in the end it's about one thing and that is making difference.

<u>Thought Prompt</u>

List reasons why you want to work with our youth:

_____

_____

_____

_____

_____

_____

_____

_____

Thought Prompt

List some potential stumbling blocks to working with our youth. Things that will have an impact on doing so in the capacity you would like. Money, time, space could be some:

_____

_____

_____

_____

What are possible solutions that may help resolve them? Look at fundraising, partnerships, or sponsorship:

_____

_____

_____

_____

*"A MAN IS FREE WHEN HE SEES HIMSELF
FOR WHAT HE IS AND NOT AS OTHERS
DEFINE HIM."*

JAMES CONE

Tip Two: Always Be Yourself

The idea of being yourself may seem like a no brainer, but for some of us it's not as easy as it sounds. In order to connect with our youth, some of us feel obligated to talk and/or act in ways we think they will relate to. The problem is many of us don't normally or usually talk and/or act in the ways of our youth. As a result, our behavior comes off forced and unnatural, which ends up undermining our ability to connect with our youth.

The question of being yourself is directly related to the question of your authenticity. In being other than yourself, you risk your authenticity, risking your authenticity puts you at risk of losing our youths' respect. Although your first inclination may be to do whatever it takes to come off as cool, it's highly likely you'll come off like a fake and phony wannabe.

Every generation has its own versions of the cool and the hip. But the hip and the cool is something we're groomed into. It kind of happens without our realizing it. We pick up words and actions in our everyday interactions with other members of our generation. Before we know it, our generation has acquired an entire way of thinking, acting, and talking that is uniquely ours. We call this amalgamation of thinking, acting, and talking subculture. Yet, because it is uniquely ours, it seems a bit foreign and odd to the generation that went before us, and outdated and corny to the generation that comes after us. It often only makes sense to us.

Being yourself may mean it will take a little longer for them to warm up to you. Your authenticity will ensure you're taken seriously and help you build stronger connections in the long run.

Now, being yourself doesn't mean that you can't or won't pick up a few things from them as you work with them. The call to be yourself at all times is a caution about forcing yourself to act and talk in ways you normally wouldn't solely for the purpose of fostering connections with our youth. By being yourself, we mean don't get caught up in pretending to be something you're not. Don't get caught up in trying to project the images you think they will relate to.

However, you should understand that over time your work with our youth will begin to influence you as much as you're going to influence them. As you find ways to connect with them without sacrificing your authenticity, you'll discover they have a wealth of insight to offer on a wide range of topics and ideas. Not to mention, working with them will also provide you an opportunity to learn more about yourself and your views on certain things. So yes, be yourself, but know that who you are will grow and change as you work with our youth.

This growth and change will occur as a result of your connecting with our youth. You don't have to change who you are or pretend to be something you're not in order to connect with our youth. You can easily relate to them by sharing you experiences. It's in sharing who you are and what you went through is where you can be yourself and be there for them too.

Listen, being other than yourself can be a major pitfall that's extremely easy to fall into. Fortunately, it's also a pitfall that's just as easily avoidable. In fact, it turns out that the question of being yourself, or not being yourself, is really a symptom or consequence of another issue: Confidence, or a lack thereof, which just happens to be the focus of our next tip.

"EXPERIENCE, WHICH DESTROY'S INNOCENCE, ALSO LEADS ONE BACK TO IT."

JAMES BALDWIN

Tip Three: Be Confident in Your "How"

Just as the question of sincerity is tied to the "why" of you're working with our youth, the question of confidence is tied to the "how" of your working with our youth. Long before you start working with our youth, you must give serious thought to how it is you're going to work with them. You're going to have to consider how you can make a difference, which means you're going to have to consider what you have to offer and how you can offer it. Thus, when we talk about confidence, we mean confidence in your ability to fulfill the role you select for yourself in working with our youth.

You need to think seriously about who you are, what you're good at, and how what you're good at can be translated into something you can offer our youth.

After doing this select a role that allows them to benefit from what it is you have to offer. Your confidence in your ability to do the thing well and your commitment at helping our youth benefit from the thing you do well dictates the nature of how our youth connect and relate to you. It reduces your inclination to rely on unauthentic ways of attempting to connect with them, such as forcing alterations to your speech and/or actions to win them over.

You need to be confident in what you're bringing to the table. If you are not confident in what it is you have to offer and your ability to offer it, how can you expect our youth to be receptive to it? Whatever role you select to play in working with our youth, you have to believe in it. You have to own it, and this ownership is much easier to achieve if you select a role that is centered around skills and/or behaviors you are confident about possessing and convinced you can translate into benefits for our youth.

Please don't confuse needing confidence with needing to be perfect. Having confidence with what you're doing should also bring ease. So no matter what situations come up, you are equipped to handle them.

Thought Prompt

List at least three skills or characteristics you have that you believe can benefit our youth:

_____

_____

_____

_____

_____

_____

_____

_____

Thought Prompt

Based on your skills and characteristics, list roles you think you can play in working with our youth (e.g. mentor, teacher, organizer):

_____

_____

_____

_____

_____

_____

_____

_____

Thought Prompt

How often would you like to engage our youth? Remember here it's not necessarily about quantity but quality.

☐ Daily (e.g. after school, classroom)

☐ Weekly (e.g. coach, ministry, club)

☐ Monthly (e.g. field trip, meetings)

☐ Yearly (e.g. annual fundraiser)

"TAKE ADVANTAGE OF EVERY OPPORTUNITY, WHERE THERE IS NONE, MAKE IT FOR YOURSELF"

MARCUS GARVEY

Tip Four: Choose Your "Where" Wisely

Just as there are many ways to work with our youth, there are a lot of places and organizations that provide an avenue for working with our youth. After considering why you want to work with our youth and how you can work with them, you're going to have to give some serious thought to where you wish to work with them. We've already mentioned the Boys and Girls Club, but there are many other programs popping up all across our nation. You can always hit the internet to find out which programs are active in your community. This brings us to the major point we want to make with regards to the "where" of your working with our youth. The closer to home, the better. The easiest way for you to make a difference with our youth is to attempt to help the youth closest to you.

If you're a parent, start at home. If you're not a parent, start with your young relatives. If you're young relatives don't actually live close enough for you to interact with them on a regular basis, interact with them as much as you can, also make an effort with the youth-aged children of friends and/or associates. If your friends and/or associates don't have any youth-aged children, try to get involved with some of the youth in your neighborhood, which may require that you volunteer at some of those formal youth programs. The point is, start.

Although starting close to home is highly practical, it also increases your potential to be effective since you have some kind of connection to build on. If it's a relative, you have the fact that you're family.

If it's a friend's kid, you have the fact that you know their parents. If it's youth from the neighborhood, you have the fact that you live in the same area. Each one of those situations presents a commonality that you can easily utilize to cultivate a connection with our youth that gives you an opportunity to make a difference in their lives.

The "where" is not just location based as to where you have to go, it is also where our youth are already spending their time. It is always easier for you to travel to them instead of hoping they can find their way to you.

If you find that in your particular area there is nothing for them to engage in, you may want to consider creating something. Again, review how much time you are willing to commit to working with them, and see how and where it fits into that schedule.

Be mindful that the closer your relative-location to the youth you're working with, the higher the level of care and concern that will drive and inspire your work with them. Furthermore, the higher your level of care and concern for the youth you're working with, the brighter your sincerity and authenticity will shine through in all your interactions with them. The question of "where" is really a question of which youth you decide to work with, and it is a question that can and will determine how effective you can be.

Thought Prompt

List places in your neighborhood where you can volunteer to engage our youth:

_____

_____

_____

_____

_____

_____

_____

_____

_____

_____

Thought Prompt

List where you can find places to interact with youths and make a difference:

_____

_____

_____

_____

_____

_____

_____

_____

_____

_____

"IT TAKES A DEEP COMMITMENT TO CHANGE AND AN EVEN DEEPER COMMITMENT TO GROW."

RALPH ELLISON

Tip Five: Active-Listening Is the Key to Effectiveness

No matter why you get involved with working with our youth. No matter how you decide to make a difference with our youth. No matter which youth you decide to work with. There is one skill you're going to have to master in order to have a real impact. You're going to have to become good at active-listening. Yes, there's something you have to offer. Yes, you're going to do your best to help our youth understand that there are alternatives to going down the wrong path. Yes, you're going to be a shining example of how doing the right thing is worth it. However, if you don't become a skilled active-listener you're probably going to botch and squander the opportunity to make a difference with our youth. You see, although whatever you have to offer our youth is important to you, as you interact with our youth they're going to reach out and tell you what's important to them. This is not to say they won't benefit from what you have to offer, but at some point they're going to make known what they really need from you. They could communicate this need directly or indirectly, what's important is that you ensure they are really comfortable with communicating their needs to you.

Thus, you need to become the kind of listener that makes them feel that they can talk to you. Unfortunately, that kind of listening is not something someone can instruct you on how to do. It takes commitment and practice. What we can do is caution you about what not to do when communicating with our youth, the avoidance of which will set you down the path to being an effective active-listener. And so we offer the following active-listening pointers:

- •Avoid Comparing
- •Avoid Mind-Reading
- •Avoid Rehearsing During a Conversation
- •Avoid Filtering
- • Avoid Prejudging
- •Avoid Sparring

Active-Listening Pointer: Avoid Comparing

Sometimes, in the midst of a conversation, we are tempted to compare what someone is saying and how they are saying it to the way we would say it or how we would say it. This kind of comparing in the midst of a conversation makes it difficult to really grasp what the person is saying because we're too busy assessing how we would have said it differently. In some cases, it's much more than how we would say things differently. It's an assessment of the other person's intelligence or emotional health in light of our own. It can result in your responding to the other person in a very condescending or pretentious manner, which can definitely ruin your chances of impacting our youth.

Avoid Comparing Tip:

Practice listening to what our youth has to say in light of who they are instead of processing everything they say in light of who you are.

Active-Listening Pointer: Avoid Mind-Reading

Mind-reading prevents us from paying attention to what people say. It's usually the result of assumptions we make about the people we're talking to. They say something that doesn't make sense in light of our preconceived assumptions, which causes us to be distrustful. As a result, we get caught up in trying to find some hidden truth behind everything the person says to us, as if everything they say is an elaborate lie. We end up paying less attention to what they are actually saying and more attention to so-called intonations and subtle cues in an effort to uncover some truth we believe to be hidden. No one wants to talk to someone who is constantly scrutinizing and distrustful of every word they say, especially our youth.

<u>Avoid Mind-Reading Tip:</u>

The best way to avoid mind-reading is by not making assumptions about the youth you're going to work with. Try your best to take what they say on face value. If and when something they say is unclear or ambiguous, kindly ask them to clarify.

Active-Listening Pointer: Avoid Rehearsing During a Conversation

It's not uncommon for us to find ourselves mentally rehearsing how we want to respond to what someone is saying while they are saying it. Unfortunately, this kind of rehearsing prevents us from paying attention to what others are saying. We don't get a chance to seriously consider what they are saying because we are too busy preparing and crafting our response.

<u>Avoid Rehearsing Tip:</u>

It's okay to have a general idea about something you're going to discuss with our youth, but listen to what they're saying, then consider everything they've said before you decide how to respond.

Focus on what they are saying, not what you are going to say.

Active-Listening Pointer: Avoid Filtering

Sometimes when someone is talking to us we find ourselves listening to some of the things they say and not to others. This is called filtering. We only pay attention to what we deem significant about what they are saying. This significance is usually signaled by certain cues: when the other person's tone indicates that they are happy or sad or about to react in a way that puts us in danger. As long as none of those things are indicated, our minds start to drift. We also filter when someone is saying something we really don't want to hear.

<u>Avoid Filtering Tip:</u>

When it comes to working with our youth, as a principle let it be a given that everything they have to say is important and worth listening to.

Active-Listening Pointer: Avoid Prejudging

Labels have enormous power, especially negative labels. Prejudging someone or something they say can cause you to pay less attention to what they say or take what they say less seriously. Hastily judging someone or something they say often results in our ceasing to listen and making knee-jerk reactions based on our prejudgments. Prejudging our youth or what it is they say can prevent us from identifying those opportunities where they are really trying to reach out to us.

Avoid Prejudging Tip:

Always remember that the reason you're working with our youth is because you believe you can make a difference in their lives. Neutralize any prejudgments you may have of whatever you perceive our youth to be; there is great potential for them to be something much more. You're trying to help them reach that potential, prejudging them and the things they say will lock them in a stagnating box.

Active-Listening Pointer: Avoid Sparring

Sometimes we have an inclination to contend with everything someone is saying to us. We call this sparring. Instead of listening to what the person is saying during a conversation, we transform the conversation into an argument or debate. We're so quick to disagree with the other person that we never hear them out. As a matter of fact, we end up focusing all our attention on finding things to contradict or disagree with. We strongly take the opposite position whenever we can.

Avoid Sparring Tip:

Before responding to anything said by our youth, take a moment to consider what they have said and then try to find at least three reasons to agree with what they've said. If you happen to have a legitimate disagreement, express it as constructively as possible. Also, consciously monitor how often you find yourself disagreeing with things said by our youth and constantly assess how you express those disagreements. Be mindful not to alienate them.

Thought Prompt

Which of the listening stumbling blocks have you fallen into in the past?
- ☐ Comparing
- ☐ Mind-Reading
- ☐ Rehearsing During a Conversation
- ☐ Filtering
- ☐ Prejudging
- ☐ Sparring

"NO ONE DOES IT ALONE."

OPRAH WINFREY

Final Thoughts

Although there are many ways for us to get involved in working with our youth, we should try to work with our youth in ways that come to us as naturally as possible. We all have something to offer our youth, we should think carefully about how we go about offering it. We all want to connect with our youth, but we shouldn't act as other than who we are in an attempt to foster those connections. We all have our own reasons for getting involved with helping our youth, we should each have a clear understanding of what those reasons are and how deeply we wish to get involved. No matter what it is we have to offer our youth, it must be offered with a heavy dose of active-listening.

The bottom line is that getting involved with our youth requires serious forethought. What is shared in this book is about inspiring and initiating the kind of forethought that leads to a serious commitment and dedication to working with our youth. It's not about what others are doing wrong with our youth; it's about what we can do right. There is no doubt that you can contribute and make a difference with our youth, you just need to take the time to carefully consider the "why," "how," and "where" of your contribution.

Once involved reinforce your commitment and look at expanding your involvement with our youth. This is not a one-time and its fixed issue. It is going to take all of us, on all levels, working together to make a difference in the lives of our youth.

ABOUT THE AUTHOR

Jamel Bragg, is a native New Yorker, who attended Park West High School in New York City. While in prison, he realized that in order for him to be a better human being, he had to change the way that he thought. Thus he began participating and completing, then later facilitating various therapeutic programs, such as:
Youth Assistance Program (a delinquent intervention program)
Alternative to Violence Project
Aggression Replacement Training
Prisoners for AIDS Counseling and Education
Residential Substance Abuse Treatment
Road to Redemption (Victim Awareness) as well as a slew of other programs

Currently he is involved in a very impacting program called Community Preparation that assists incarcerated men with their reintegration back into society.

He is also is working on his second non-fiction book titled: *Saving our Community One Block at a Time.*

It's his hope to take his experiences as well as the information that he has learned and bring it to the inner city youths to show them that change is possible.

If you are interested in getting in contact with the author for speaking engagements, seminars or comments, contact him at:
info@prestigecommunicationgroup.com.